Crystals & ENERGIES

Claire Taupin

THE WITCH'S APPRENTICE

Crystals & ENERGIES

The essential witch's kit for using
crystals to find balance and well-being

Hardie Grant

QUADRILLE

Table of contents

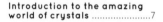

You've chosen your stones, what next?

Making the stones your own

How to work with your stone

Cleansing

Recharging

Storage

SOS, my stone is gone!

My crystal emergency kit

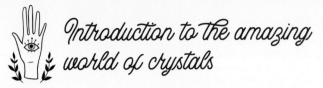

Introduction to the amazing world of crystals

Hello and welcome to the amazing world of crystals and energies! I think it's best to warn you now: you are entering an incredibly vibrant universe where you will discover a lot about the world, other people and yourself. Ready?

Before we start, I just want to point out that you are going to read the words "stones" and "crystals" very often. I use both terms throughout the book, but they have the same meaning! These small stones, which all carry a different energy that resonates with our own, have always fascinated me... When I was a child, I carried a blue agate around with me. It was my lucky charm. It is considered to be the stone of inner peace. What a lovely coincidence!

When I started looking online for a natural solution to my anxiety attacks, I heard about lithotherapy, which is therapy using crystals. Conventional medicine was not the answer to my emotional distress and I knew it. But I felt comforted when I carried a blue calcite, an extremely calming stone that helps to prevent anxiety attacks and is said to make them less severe when they do occur.

Since then, every day, I wear natural stone bracelets depending on my energy at the time, my needs and my desires... Sometimes I wear the same stones for several weeks so that their energy can take root in me and to allow them to do in-depth work. Sometimes I also change bracelets during the day. When I go on a trip, I have a pharmacy kit and... a witch's kit. I take my crystals with me in case I feel anxious, demotivated or not anchored in the present moment.

A few years ago, I was searching the internet for a monthly subscription box with stones. There weren't any, so I wanted to offer one myself! I created a subscription box, hence the name of my company, Mysticbox, in which I offer several crystals and explanations to understand them, all based on the lunar cycle of the current month. I read a great deal about stones, attended conferences about lithotherapy and consulted lithotherapists and magnetisers – while carefully respecting the limit between selling stones with some advice and offering a treatment with the stones. It was important to me that I help others discover what I had discovered a few years ago, but for the time being, my goal is not to be a healer. Today, I have a brick-and-mortar shop in Ancenis (Loire-Atlantique, France) and an online shop with natural stones: *Mysticbox.fr*. I guide my clients in their choice of crystals on a daily basis.

This book is not intended to make you an expert – I don't think any book could make such a claim when it comes to this subject! But the goal is that once you have finished reading it, you will be able to listen to your personal energy, identify which of your chakras are not working properly and choose one or more stones to "heal" your energy.

Before
you get
STARTED

How do crystals work?

All crystals carry an energy inside them. This energy, which is different for each of them, comes in contact with your own energy. It is divided among your seven main chakras and, depending on their general balance, enables you to feel good or not. Stones will never hurt you, but they can create an imbalance or maintain a pre-existing imbalance. That's why it is important to first examine your feelings and understand how the energy circulating in your body works.

1. THE IMPORTANCE OF CHAKRAS

Chakras are energy centres that can be found all along your spinal column. There are seven main chakras. To visualise them in your mind, you can imagine spirals of wind spinning quickly or slowly:

✦ **A balanced chakra** contains a spiral of wind that is clearly present but not excessive.

✦ **A weak chakra** is like a very gentle breeze.

✦ **An overdeveloped chakra** cannot contain the wind any longer. It is too powerful and too chaotic, and it spins too quickly.

When our chakras are out of balance, we experience strong or weak symptoms in our body or behaviour. Some of our chakras can even be blocked. The goal is to maintain a certain balance so that the energy circulates freely.

The energy of the crystals that you wear on your body or that you keep around you (as long as they are big enough) will resonate with one or more of these chakras to promote balanced spinning.

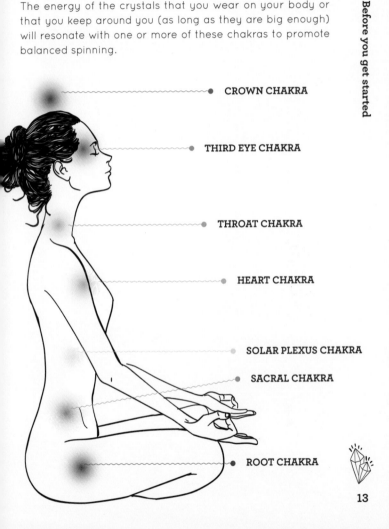

CROWN CHAKRA

THIRD EYE CHAKRA

THROAT CHAKRA

HEART CHAKRA

SOLAR PLEXUS CHAKRA

SACRAL CHAKRA

ROOT CHAKRA

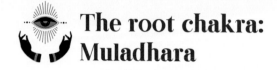

The root chakra: Muladhara

Meaning: "Root"
Also called the "base" chakra, it is located at the bottom of the spine. It allows us to feel at home in our physical body, to live in the present moment. It is also responsible for the skeleton, the colon, the genital organs and health in general.

�֍ **Balanced chakra:** We feel anchored in a good way, at home in our body, healthy, full of energy. Our life is stable and generally organised.

✖ **Weak chakra:** We are anxious, unsatisfied, regularly sick, physically weak, we feel insecure. We overthink things, we put everything off until tomorrow, we are disorganised, disconnected from reality.

✖ **Overdeveloped chakra:** We are too rooted in our habits. It is hard for us to change even the littlest things, we feel stiff and inflexible. We accumulate things due to the fear of not having enough, we feel vulnerable when we are not in control.

Crystals that can help

Those that are red (red jasper, red agate, garnet, red carnelian, etc.), brown (tiger's eye, bull's eye, brown agate, brown jasper) and black (tourmaline, onyx).

The sacral chakra: Svadhisthana

Meaning: "Where your being is established"
The second chakra is located in the lower abdomen, under the navel. It allows us to experience emotions and enjoy physical pleasure. It regulates sexuality, creativity and the sacred feminine. It is associated with the entire pelvic area, the lower back, the bladder and the kidneys.

★ **Balanced chakra:** We feel pleasure, we appreciate life and we take advantage of it, we accept change. We are comfortable with our sexuality and we enjoy it, we are carried along by the flow of life.

★ **Weak chakra:** We feel divorced from our bodies, passive, cold, distant and disconnected. We easily feel lonely, we don't like our bodies and we feel uncomfortable with our sexuality.

★ **Overdeveloped chakra:** We are on a constant roller-coaster of emotions, our creativity is completely blocked. We have problems with addictions, a tendency to be egocentric, to think only of our own pleasure.

Crystals that can help

Those that are orange (carnelian, orange calcite, citrine, adular moonstone, amber, etc.).

15

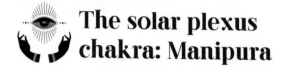

The solar plexus chakra: Manipura

Meaning: "That which shines"
As its name implies, Manipura is located in the upper abdomen at the level of the solar plexus. It regulates personal power and self-confidence. It is also the chakra of the ego, objectives, limits and intuition. It is related to the stomach, liver, diaphragm and immune system.

★ **Balanced chakra:** We feel energetic, sure of ourselves, precise, focused. We are assertive, we show the world our value, we shine, we trust our intuition and we act.

★ **Weak chakra:** We have trouble making decisions, we are afraid to excel. We are relatively passive, or even submissive, we are the victim of our own life, we lack ambition.

★ **Overdeveloped chakra:** We work too much, we are arrogant or perfectionists in the extreme sense of the word. We are easily angered, we have strong, disproportionate reactions and problems with addiction.

Crystals that can help

Those that are yellow (citrine, yellow calcite, tiger's eye, yellow fluorite, amber, etc.).

The heart chakra: Anahata

Meaning: "Infinite sound, eternal and universal love"
Located in the centre of the chest, Anahata speaks of unconditional love, compassion for yourself and for others, joy, forgiveness, and letting go... It's also the chakra that connects the three lower chakras to the three upper chakras. Some people say that all energy comes from there. It is responsible for the heart, lungs, upper back and legs.

★ **Balanced chakra:** We view the world and other people with kindness, we are gentle and kind to ourselves. We know how to protect ourselves from the suffering of others while remaining empathetic. We know how to forgive, we are at peace with ourselves and we enjoy life.

★ **Weak chakra:** We have a hard time giving and receiving love. We have low self-esteem, we think we are undeserving. We are resentful, we feel lonely, we are very affected by criticism.

★ **Overdeveloped chakra:** We are extremely sensitive. We can't stand the idea of being involved in conflicts. We are impatient, exhausted from having given too much. We may also be co-dependent.

Crystals that can help

Those that are green (aventurine, jade, chrysoprase, malachite, amazonite, etc.) and those that are pink (pink quartz, rhodonite, rhodochrosite, etc.).

17

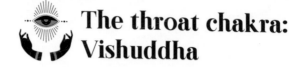

The throat chakra: Vishuddha

Meaning: "Purification, clarity"
Vishuddha, located in the throat and at the nape of the neck, is the centre of communication, truth and the ability to listen. This chakra is responsible for the nape of the neck, throat, shoulders, mouth, sinuses and ears.

★ **Balanced chakra:** We talk to others in a respectful way. We manage to express our thoughts, we dare to say no when we don't agree, we know how to listen to others and we also know how to appreciate silence.

★ **Weak chakra:** We have a hard time expressing ourselves. Sometimes we're shy or have a hushed voice, we run away from conflict and disagreements, we don't dare say no. We have difficulty expressing our own ideas.

★ **Overdeveloped chakra:** We talk non-stop, we have a hard time listening to others, a tendency to interrupt, to tease others. We gossip and talk negatively about other people behind their backs.

Crystals that can help

Those that are sky blue (angelite, blue chalcedony, aquamarine, amazonite, etc.).

The third eye chakra: Ajna

Meaning: "To perceive"
The sixth chakra is located between the two eyebrows. It represents the sixth sense, intuition, spiritual consciousness, wisdom, clairvoyance, the ability to see the long-term consequences, to distance ourselves from a situation. It controls the eyes, brain and pineal gland.

★ **Balanced chakra:** We are able to look beyond small, everyday problems, our vision is clear. Our connection to the invisible world is clear and established, we know how to listen to our intuition and follow its messages. We have a good balance between reality and feelings.

★ **Weak chakra:** We are overly focused on reality and lose contact with our inner-self. We are disconnected from any spirituality, we have a hard time being creative and accepting the opinions of others. We don't see any magic in everyday life anymore.

★ **Overdeveloped chakra:** We see signs from the Universe all the time and everywhere. We often feel overwhelmed or lost. We have an over-active imagination and we are disconnected from reality.

Crystals that can help

Those that are dark blue (sodalite, lapis lazuli, azurite, etc.) and those that are purple (amethyst, lepidolite, purple fluorite, etc.).

19

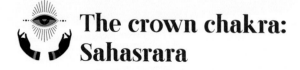

The crown chakra: Sahasrara

Meaning: "A thousand petals"
Represented by an infinite lotus and located at the top of the head in our energy aura, Sahasrara enables us to connect to the divine, to everything that cannot be explained, to the invisible world, to energies! It is also associated with the brain and the pituitary gland.

★ **Balanced chakra:** We are comfortable in our human condition, connected to something greater than ourselves. We are able to feel awe, to find meaning in life. We have a healthy detachment from material things.

★ **Weak chakra:** We are hostile to spirituality or we have the feeling that we are deeply cut off from it. We can't find any meaning in life, we tend to over-consume. We feel very alone and depressed.

★ **Overdeveloped chakra:** We are completely disconnected from reality, we aren't in our physical body anymore. We are sometimes even subject to spiritual or religious fanaticism that can turn into delusions.

Crystals that can help

Those that are white (howlite, milky quartz, etc.) those that are purple (amethyst, lepidolite, purple fluorite, etc.) and those that are transparent (rock crystal).

2. CAN STONES BE USED FOR CHILDREN?

The recommendations in this book can apply to children as well, as long as they are old enough to look after their stones, are supervised using them and aren't at risk of swallowing any crystals (or choking on them), of course. But in principle the work done with stones and chakras is the same as for adults. We often notice children who are attracted by one stone in particular in the shop. I think it is good to listen to their intuition and remember that the stone they have chosen will certainly be a source of learning and well-being for them. Of course, you can also select a stone based on the issues your child is dealing with, or ask for advice. If you can, don't hesitate to take your child to a specialised shop in person.

3. AND WHAT ABOUT PETS?

Pets also have chakras; it is therefore absolutely possible to work with stones. But be careful, a few rules of caution are necessary: don't choose a stone that could be swallowed by animals, watch  out for salt stones as they can be licked (e.g. salt lamp or selenite). Since animals can't speak, you will have to understand what is right or wrong for them. The right way to go about this is to place the stone in the place where your pet sleeps. If they leave this area, it's probably because the stone is not a good match for them.

21

Where should I buy my stones?

Today, many places sell crystals: specialised shops, stands at markets, bookshops, online stores, and even at shops that are NOT SUITABLE AT ALL – I have seen stones for sale at a cooking utensil shop and in a tobacco shop! It can be very confusing, and it's good to be discerning, since not all stones are of the same quality.

1. IN A SHOP

Ideally, you should go to a shop that specialises in the sale of fine stones and minerals. An internet search will allow you find those that are local to you. Going directly to the shop has several advantages:

★ A salesperson (who is very likely to be passionate about crystals!) will answer your questions and help you make a choice.

★ In the vast majority of shops, you can see and touch the stones.

★ You will be able to find out about their origin.

Sustainable and ethical mining practices

The stone trade is unfortunately very opaque. It is difficult to trace stones' origin and to be completely sure that they come from a place where people and Nature are treated with respect. It is important to keep in mind that crystals, despite how abundant they may seem, are precious. They are gifts that Nature guards jealously, hidden deep inside

LABEL MINES RAISONNÉES

rocks. To obtain these crystals, the rock that imprisons them must be destroyed. In most cases, this extraction is done using large amounts of explosives, under deplorable conditions for workers.

The stones that I sell in my online and brick-and-mortar shops have earned the French "Mines Raisonnées" certification that ensures that the supplier pays close attention to the way in which the crystals are obtained (a broad topic that deserves its own book!) and the way in which the workers are treated at the site. Most of these stones come from South America. Companies that require this certification often post it in their shop, as a selling point! If not, there is a strong chance that the stones come from other sources.

2. ONLINE

It is of course possible to buy crystals online if there are no shops near you. However, you can't choose the exact stone yourself, which may be a problem for some people.

As for my online shop, I take the time to be "called" by a stone when I am preparing each client's order. I often receive messages when my clients receive the packages such as: "My stone is magnificent! It is exactly the size of my thumb", or "It has a little black spot, I love it! That makes it unique. It's probably the one I would have chosen myself!" I strongly believe that when you order from a trusted website, you receive the stone that is right for you.

On the other hand, I strongly advise against buying from (very) cheap websites. This usually means that child labour has been used and/or the working conditions are inhumane. I am convinced that stones extracted under these conditions cannot offer their best energy. A stone is precious; it's understandable that it has to cost a certain amount.

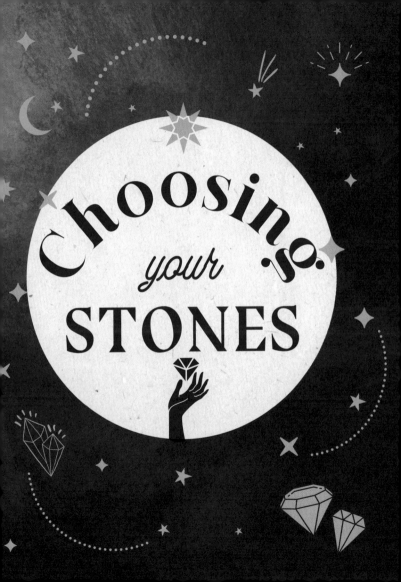

Choosing your STONES

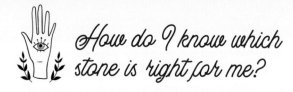

How do I know which stone is right for me?

The first and probably most important thing to remember is that there is no wrong answer to this question. Relax, rid yourself of any pressure you may feel and don't worry about making a mistake: The stone that you choose will always have something positive to offer you.

1. FOLLOW YOUR INTUITION

The first way to choose a stone is to simply go to a shop and let the stone call you. You will think that one stone is more beautiful than the others, notice it among all the others, and it will be THE ONE. Intuition can be like a little voice in your head or a feeling that runs through your body. Whatever the case may be, this feeling can be somewhat fleeting. For example, if you feel "called" to an amethyst, take it in your hands and if you start thinking "well, yes, but...", then you've already forgotten your intuition. Intuition doesn't negotiate, it doesn't look for an explanation, it informs, it knows. As soon as you are thinking "yes, but", it's your brain talking.

In my opinion, a stone that is chosen by intuition will always have something to offer you. It is actually quite amazing to go home, open your book on the subject and read the description of the stone you chose. The reaction is usually overwhelming: "It's EXACTLY the one I needed!"

2. SEEK ADVICE FROM A SPECIALIST

You can also visit a lithotherapist or reputable salesperson. Explain your problem; the specialist will direct you towards one or several suitable stones. This is an excellent practice that you can implement from time to time, particularly if you're dealing with a fear or a phobia, in which case your intuition may have trouble guiding you. This is because fear prevents us from moving towards the stones that could be useful to us; we can even feel repelled by them!

Lithotherapist or salesperson?

It is important to note the difference between these two professions. The person who sells the stones fully understands their virtues and the chakras and often works with his or her intuition to advise you. You can ask this person questions and receive relevant answers about your personal issues. The lithotherapist is perfectly capable of giving you the same answers and advising you in your choice of crystals. But, as the name implies, the lithotherapist's objective is to heal. He or she can truly rebalance your energies using crystals.

3. BY COLOUR OR MINDFUL REFLECTION

Another method is to connect with your chakras, studying the ones that are out of balance and identifying the stones of the right colour that are meant for your problem in particular. Don't be afraid of making a mistake in this case, either. You know yourself; you are more capable than anyone else of knowing what you need.

Can I work with several stones at the same time?

I really like to work with stone "synergies", meaning a set of several stones used for the same reason (see pages 42–56 for a few examples of synergies). Remember that covering yourself from head to toe with stones will not help you, and could even work against you. Our energy body is unable to handle too much information at once. That's why I usually name three stones, or up to five stones if all of them are used to treat the same problem and act on the same chakra.

You also have to use common sense: if you feel tired or need to rest, wearing jasper, for example, which will encourage you to get moving and start working on your projects, is probably not the best idea. It would be better to choose rose quartz, to take care of yourself and have a break.

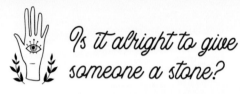

Is it alright to give someone a stone?

Yes! Of course, you can give someone a stone as a gift. It's a very nice thing to do. It's a gift that has meaning, that offers an energy renewal, a feeling of wellness, help with concentration, or any other property that is part of the work done with crystals. What a lovely idea!

1. HOW TO CHOOSE IT

Once you're in a shop, you can make your selection based on your intuition. Ask yourself which stone calls to you for this gift. You can also trust your knowledge of the person. Is it hard for them to make time for themselves? Give them rose quartz to help them focus on themselves. Is your loved one starting a company and you want to support them and wish them good luck? Jasper or citrine could be just right! Does the recipient tell you that they often have nightmares? Then amethyst would be excellent!

When it comes to the shape of the stone, I would say that it depends mainly on how much you want to spend.

2. LET THEM DECIDE

It is essential that you tell the person receiving the gift that he or she must feel completely free to wear or carry it OR NOT. It is an energy helper, not a traditional gift. The stone will have an impact on the person carrying it and the recipient must feel comfortable in contact with this energy, and attracted to the idea of carrying it on his or her person. Make sure that you take the time to explain all of this to them. It is very important not to feel obligated to wear a crystal simply because you don't want to hurt or disappoint the person giving it.

And what if I'm not sure?

If you feel too unsure about choosing a stone for someone else, but you would really like to give them one, you might want to consider a gift card. Most shops offer them. This will allow your loved one to choose the stone that calls to them the most.

Does the shape of the stone have an impact on its energy?

The shape of the stones that you choose to accompany you in your energy work has an impact. It determines, to a certain extent, the way in which each stone will communicate with your energy. The first big distinction to make is between raw stones, which have undergone very little processing, and processed stones.

1. RAW STONES

The energy of these stones is "pure", as nothing has altered them. However, they are not necessarily better: it is possible to work just as effectively with a tumbled stone (see page 38) as with a raw stone. Remember, the objective of this book is to support you in your choice, not to force you to act in any particular way. Your intuition, your feeling and your opinion are real guides that deserve your attention more than anything else.

Raw stones are often less expensive than cut or tumbled stones, because they required less work. Let's take the example of rose quartz, a stone that is full of gentleness. It would probably be cheaper to purchase a large piece of raw stone so that its energy can fill the whole room rather than a big piece of polished rose quartz. Beyond the financial aspect, raw stones either attract or repel, depending on the person. Listen to yourself. Personally, I love raw stones; as I'm writing these lines, that's all I have on my desk!

2. TUMBLED STONES

These are the stones that you will mostly find in various specialised brick-and-mortar shops and online. Tumbled stones are raw stones that have been placed in a barrel containing abrasive sand and water, which rub away the irregularities as the barrel is turned, transforming them into perfectly smooth stones. In my opinion, tumbled stones are the easiest stones to work with. Their energy is gentle, you can take them everywhere and they feel good to touch. Tumbled stones are sold from about £1.70 or $2.20; an excellent way to work with stones for very little investment. The other advantage is that crystal shops often have a wide variety of tumbled stones, so there will definitely be one (or several) for you!

3. CUT STONES

These stones have been processed to have various properties. For example, someone may want the stone to end in a point (as in the picture opposite). Witches believe that the point conducts the energy that comes from the Universe, bringing it into the crystal and thus closer to you. A double point promotes the exchange of energy, the passage from one object or one person to the next. You can also find **moon-shaped stones**, as the moon is the symbol of sacred female energy; **round stones**, which promote harmony; and **heart-shaped stones**, which encourage goodwill.

What would I recommend when choosing this type of stone? Trust yourself. Ideally, go to a shop. The feeling that passes between you and the stone is very important in this case. These stones have been heavily processed, so they often cost more: a rock crystal double point, for example, will range between £8.50/$11 and £25/$33 depending on the size. Even a small stone cut into a moon or star shape will

cost more than a tumbled stone: for example, it may cost between £12.50/$16.50 and £25/$33.

4. STONES MADE INTO JEWELLERY

Stones can be made into jewellery, either as pendants or beads that are then strung as bracelets, malas (types of large necklaces composed of 108 beads, used during meditation to count breaths), necklaces, rings, etc. They are both useful and fun. This is the type of stone that I work with most of the time. Choosing my bracelets in the morning has become a real ritual!

Some settings are better than others. For example, a pink or green stone that you wear near your heart, even if it is small, will bring precious support energy to your body. The same is true if you wear a sky blue stone near your throat. The placement of these stones at certain locations on the body is important, and jewellery can be an excellent way to work on each chakra very precisely. Another example would be wearing a citrine pendant near the solar plexus, the chakra of our radiance, perfect for self-confidence!

Another advantage of stones worn as jewellery: in addition to taking advantage of their energy, you are aware of them. During the day, you will hear your bracelet rub against the desk or you will feel the chain holding the pendant moving on your neck. This is a constant reminder that your stones are supporting you and to live mindfully in the present moment.

Is there a difference between small and large stones?

Yes and no! No, since the energy of a stone will be the same regardless of whether it is large or small. A small carnelian will offer the same beneficial properties as a larger one. But yes, since a small stone will only diffuse this energy for a few centimetres around itself. That's why small tumbled stones are good allies for everyday use, to be kept in your pocket. On the other hand, a small stone placed on your coffee table will not have any effect on the room.

41

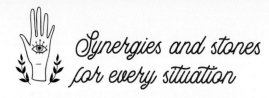

Synergies and stones for every situation

In my shop, I welcome new people every day who often have similar obstructions. Below is a list of some of the most common problems that I encounter.

1. "I DON'T SLEEP WELL OR I HAVE TROUBLE FALLING ASLEEP"

Sleep problems, which are extremely common, often occur when the wheels of our mind won't stop spinning, even at night. The synergy that I suggest here acts on the heart chakra and on the upper chakras (third eye and crown) to help your mind get the rest it deserves.

The synergy is composed of the following stones (which you can see in the picture on the right):

✦ **Amethyst:** eases the mind, helps to calm you, promotes peaceful thoughts.

✦ **Rose quartz:** tempers the properties of the amethyst and diffuses energy that is full of gentleness, enabling you to feel confident when falling asleep. It helps balance your emotions and reassures the wearer.

✦ **Lepidolite:** enables restorative sleep and prevents nightmares. It has an in-depth effect on stress and anxiety.

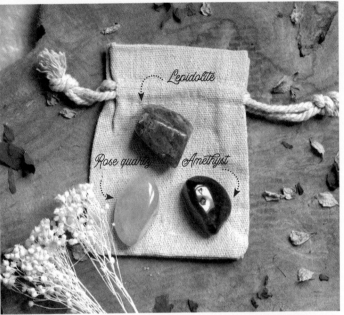

Lepidolite

Rose quartz   Amethyst

A witch's advice to help you sleep

Before going to sleep, ask yourself: "What benefits will sleep bring to me?" Really connect with the answer – physical rest, energy for tomorrow, mental clarity, feeling of freedom, etc.

2. "I LACK SELF-CONFIDENCE, I FEEL BAD ABOUT MYSELF"

This is probably one of the obstructions that affects the widest range of people: children, teens, young adults, older people, women and men. None of us seem to be immune from these thoughts, which can crop up at any time. And for a good reason: in this age of social media where appearances and looks seem to matter most, where we compare ourselves to everyone else, it is easy to doubt ourselves. This blockage is located in the solar plexus chakra.

The synergy is composed of the following stones:

✦ **Natural citrine:** this is the stone of abundance. It promotes deep self-confidence by rebalancing the solar plexus chakra. Its energy is invigorating, it brings joy and creativity and stimulates self-expression. It also keeps away self-destructive thoughts.

✦ **Yellow calcite:** very energising and purifying, it helps us go beyond our fears and allows us to believe in our own potential. It makes us feel better, calms the spirit and replaces emotional stress with serenity.

✦ **Haematite:** anchors us in the present moment and encourages us to respect ourselves. It allows us to exceed the limits that others have imposed on us and to consider failure as a kind of learning. It communicates true self-confidence.

Yellow calcite

Natural citrine

Haematite

A witch's advice to gain self-confidence

Every day, write down three positive things about yourself
in your favourite notebook: a personality trait, a physical
attribute, a professional skill, etc. It can be anything, as long
as it is positive. Do this for three weeks to reinforce your
solar plexus chakra.

3. "I HAVE ANXIETY ATTACKS"

As I explained in the introduction, this is the problem that led me to use stones in the first place. An anxiety attack is a particularly unpleasant and paralysing feeling. Generally without any apparent reason (except for those invented in your own mind), you suddenly feel that you are going to die or that something extremely bad is going to happen.

The synergy is composed of the following stones:

✦ **Smoky quartz:** anchors its wearer to the ground and to the present moment, by helping you get a grip on your thoughts and mental images. It makes it possible to get through the attack by conveying a certain firmness: NO, nothing bad is happening. Your determination is boosted and the negative energy circulating inside of you is replaced by positive energy.

✦ **Sodalite:** promotes rational thought, objectivity and the search for truth, everything you need to prevent an anxiety attack from occurring. It soothes the mind and allows the heart to let go of its fears. It is especially recommended in case of phobias.

Sodalite

Smoky quartz

A witch's advice to calm anxiety attacks

Begin some *shadow work*: take the time to sit down and search for what is hiding behind your anxiety attacks. What triggers them? What are you really afraid of? Always ask yourself: "Why?" You will dig up insecurities that can be managed by talking about them.

4. "I AM STRESSED OUT AND ANXIOUS"

Since the word "stress" covers many situations, some introspective work is necessary to understand what is hiding behind this stress before choosing a stone. This will allow you to explain your stress using different words and to talk about it with a specialist, who will therefore be able to point you in the right direction. The group of stones proposed here helps to combat anxiety in general, when we don't ever really feel calm, or when we always feel worried...

The synergy is composed of the following stones:

✦ **Rose quartz:** this is the stone of tenderness, love and self-love. It calms us when we are emotional and brings a lot of gentleness to daily life and relationships. It offers a feeling of serenity.

✦ **Rhodochrosite:** soothes anger, resentment, judgement and emotionality. It calms the physical effects of stress (stomach ache, palpitations etc.). It drives out parasitic and repetitive thoughts that keep us in a state of constant stress.

✦ **Howlite:** deeply calming and stabilising. It dispels fears and helps us bring our spirit and our feelings into harmony. It allows us to let go of emotional fears and to take responsibility for achieving our well-being.

Other stones are also suitable for working on this problem, including: blue calcite, aquamarine, sodalite, smoky quartz, pyrite, chrysoprase, amethyst, moonstone, onyx, blue chalcedony, rhodonite and angelite. It is important to do some introspective work! The Crystal Emergency Kit on pages 90–137 will also give you some tips on understanding these stones and which ones could help you.

A witch's advice to combat anxiety

Anxiety is dispelled through action, so write, paint, work out, tidy up, go gardening! Work on mindfulness as well. Focus your attention on your action RIGHT NOW. If you meditate, or if you would like to reconnect to the present without "doing" anything, then focus on your breathing, or on what each of your five senses is experiencing.

Rose quartz

Rhodochrosite

Howlite

5. "I'M SHY / I HAVE A HARD TIME EXPRESSING MYSELF"

Shyness or difficulty expressing oneself, speaking in public or joining a group can be very incapacitating in daily life. The synergy that I'm suggesting here is oriented towards communication. It allows you to rebalance the throat chakra. If the shyness is coupled with a significant lack of self-confidence, don't hesitate to add yellow stones.

The synergy is composed of the following stones:

★ **Aquamarine:** this stone counters stress, calms the mind, keeps away superfluous thoughts, gets you moving and hones the intellect. If you tend to stammer or not find the right words, it is ideal! It gets rid of confusion and promotes personal expression.

★ **Blue chalcedony:** offers verbal dexterity and optimism. It makes it possible to stimulate the gift of listening and communication. It improves your self image when speaking in public and dispels negative thoughts.

A witch's advice to rebalance the throat chakra

Sing! In the shower, in the car, in the street! Sing... wherever you feel like it! Don't try and get out of it by saying: "I sing off-key/badly". The objective is to release your energy. You can even chant mantras if you like.

6. "I WANT TO PROTECT MYSELF AGAINST NEGATIVE ENERGIES"

According to the beliefs of witches, when one starts to connect with the invisible world, doors are opened. When this happens, we give free reign to very positive energies, to our intuition, from our guides, from the Universe – call them whatever you would like. But these doors can also allow more negative energies to enter, which come from spiritual realms but also from the people around us (be they strangers or friends and family). We have to protect ourselves and stay anchored by seeking spiritual protection.

The synergy is composed of the following stones:

★ **Black tourmaline:** the anchoring stone of the synergy. Spiritual growth can't happen without a solid footing. Before reconnecting with your soul, we must be present in, love and protect our physical body. That's what tourmaline is for. It also reinforces full consciousness and peace of mind.

★ **Labradorite:** the stone of spiritual protection that you need when you connect with your spirituality. It acts as a true energy shield against negative energy from other people. In addition to this mental protection, it helps you to develop clairvoyance and to connect with your intuition.

A witch's advice to protect yourself

Lighting a candle when you connect to these spiritual realms allows you to keep a connection to the light. When you complete a ritual, purifying the energies with sage can be a good habit (see page 75).

7. "I HAVE A HARD TIME GETTING THINGS DONE/I PUT EVERYTHING OFF UNTIL TOMORROW"

The hardest thing about getting certain projects done, such as organising administrative papers or any other seemingly boring task, is taking the first step. Once you have taken this step, everything else follows. Grab this group of stones when you lack motivation – don't have any others on your person – and allow yourself to be carried by this energy of vitality and action!

The synergy is composed of the following stones:

★ **Red jasper:** the stone for getting things done. Jasper allows us to dare, to take the first step. It offers courage, strength and considerable motivation to tackle problems. It's also THE anti-procrastination crystal. It wakes up our brain and body. Finally, it enables us to imagine the future of our projects and better plan for their completion.

★ **Mookaite jasper:** this other type of jasper increases efficiency. It allows us to do many things in a short amount of time. It helps us to have new ideas and a different outlook on our work. It helps us launch into projects with enthusiasm (from the renovation of a cottage to the creation of your own company).

★ **Tiger's eye:** the stone for concentration. It encourages us to take mindful action and promotes self-confidence. It allows us to see obstacles as opportunities to go further and helps us get up and go!

★ **Carnelian:** the stone for good habits. It enables us to change old habits and to make new ones. It offers momentum, vitality and energy. It increases creativity and reinforces memory.

Mookaite jasper

Red jasper

Tiger's eye

Carnelian

A witch's advice to taking action

Work on your fear of failure. A lack of confidence in one's abilities can often create the fear to try: we subconsciously prefer putting things off rather than being confronted with not being good enough. And even supposing you aren't very good at whatever you're trying, remember that life is a constant learning experience!

53

8. "I WANT TO DEVELOP MY INTUITION/I WANT TO CONNECT WITH MY INNER WITCH"

If you are reading these words, it's safe to say that the "witch" inside of you is already wide awake. This synergy will therefore support you in the work that you have already started. It will help you connect to spiritual realms, the Universe, Nature and the Invisible world.

The synergy is composed of the following stones:

✦ **Amethyst:** the sorcerer's stone. It allows us to connect with our intuition and our subtle perceptions. It is absolutely necessary to have it on your person to learn to put your brain on pause, to allow yourself to rest.

✦ **Moonstone:** if you are a woman, this stone helps you connect with your cycle and to bring out all its power. It also offers precious guidance when experiencing our emotions, through which you can be sure that you will receive messages – for example, to refuse the invitation to that dinner because you want to have time for yourself, or on the other hand, the desire to seize an opportunity even if it means leaving your comfort zone. Your emotions can tell you all of this, if you give them the opportunity.

✦ **Fluorite:** a very protective stone that cleanses and reorganises the body's energies and intensifies the connection of the bearer to spiritual energies. It is an important ally when learning about feelings and during rituals.

A witch's advice to help develop your intuition

There's so much to say! Read, dive into the subjects that interest you the most, get carried away by a new subject, work with your stones, of course! Spend time with Nature, recharge your batteries in her presence, learn from her! Try meditation. Allow yourself some time alone. Write every day. Perform rituals. Participate in a moon circle - this involves coming together with other people during the full moon or the new moon to honour Nature and your cyclic rhythm, using dances, songs, writing or any other practice that appeals to you.

55

9. "I HAVE A DIFFERENT PROBLEM"

Of course, this list is far from exhaustive, but the information about the chakras in the first chapter (see pages 12–25) and the descriptions of each stone that you will find in the pages that follow will provide everything you need to identify the stone(s) that are important for you right now.

My advice: Take the time to understand which chakra(s) are related to your problem. Once you have done this, determine the colour associated with the chakra(s), then the corresponding stones. Then you can make your selection.

Can I work with a stone just for the fun of it?

I talk a lot about problems here because that's often what guides the purchase of a crystal. However, nothing prevents you from choosing a stone without knowing anything about it, because you think it's beautiful, because its energy attracts you... Or from wearing it to work with it, without any problem in particular!

Making the stones your own

All right, you bought your stones! You probably purchased several, maybe you even gave in and bought a piece of jewellery. I get it, when I bought my first crystals, I wanted to buy the whole shop. I am also willing to bet that between the shop and your home, you touched and looked at your stones, and felt a certain well-being or pleasure at the idea of diving into this new subject...

1. THE POWER OF INTENTION

As in any witch's work or ritual, the intention that you place in your stone is very powerful. Most importantly, know that it is not mandatory or necessary to work with stones, but it is a practice that I highly recommend!

The intention is usually related to the reason why you selected this stone. For example, you bought a sodalite to calm your anxiety attacks. Your intention could be (reformulate with your words and for your problems): "This sodalite will be the stone that I will hold whenever I feel my stress level rising." There you have it, your stone contains your intention. You can make this into a ritual by lighting a candle, burning incense or maybe writing down your feelings in a notebook (see the box on page 64). But again, this is not mandatory! Simply taking your stone and thinking very hard about your intention is enough.

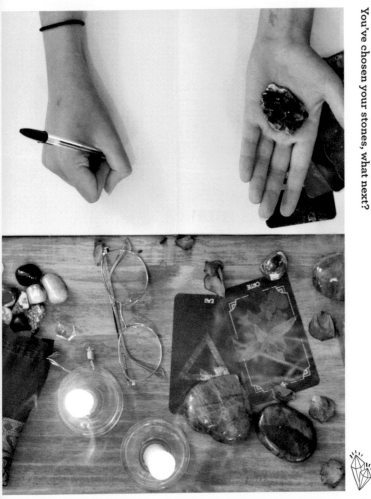

2. CONNECTING WITH THE STONE'S ENERGY

I'm sure you've got it by now... we work with stones for the energies that they carry and we should take the time to welcome them. Even more so if you are just beginning to work with crystals! To do this, I recommend sitting on the ground in a comfortable position with your back nice and straight, which is essential for properly feeling the energies. Remember that your seven main chakras are located up and down your spine. If you feel any pain, feel free to sit against a wall, or even on a chair (in which case you must keep both feet on the ground and not cross your legs).

Contact with the ground is important: by being aware of your connection with the ground and your crystal, you activate your root chakra (see page 14). This base must be solid in order to support all the other chakras. Once you are seated, close your eyes, take a few breaths to centre yourself and hold your stone in your hands. Let your intuition speak to you. Yes, this is a little vague, but it is the best advice I can give you. Your feelings will be different from those of other people. You may see a colour when you close your eyes, feel a reassuring presence, a tingling in different parts of your body, an energy that rises up along your spine, shivers, heat or cold, etc. Welcome these sensations, everything that you feel is good.

If nothing happens, do not make any judgements about yourself or your crystal. Sometimes it takes a little time to make a connection. Try it without any particular expectation. The less you expect, the more you will be ready to listen. The ego has no place here. There are no "good" or "bad" feelings, no comparisons to be made. Be curious and open.

The written word

Why not write down your feelings in a notebook? This can be the chance to create a shadow book, a witch's spell book that contains your thoughts, recipes, feelings, etc. You can have a look at this notebook in a few months or a few years and compare what you wrote down at different times. I love to reread my notes from the first times I worked with crystals – it's fascinating and it shows how much my practice has improved.

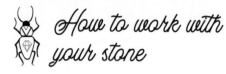

How to work with your stone

Regardless of the personal work you are doing with your crystals, it is necessary to carry them. Buying a small tumbled stone and leaving it in a cup in the bathroom is useless: you have to carry it on your person and be in contact with its energy body. Remember, working with two to four stones at once is enough: be careful not to create an energy "hubbub".

1. I TAKE MY CUES FROM THE STONE'S SHAPE

The intention has been stated, your connection is established, you have officially started working with your stone, the size of which determines the best way to proceed on a daily basis (for more information about stone shapes, see pages 36 to 41).

"My stone is small or it's a piece of jewellery"

In this case, wear it or carry it with you in your pocket, with as much contact with your skin as possible. If it is very small, putting it in your purse will have no effect.

"My stone is large and/or raw"

You can place it in a strategic location. If you purchase carnelian to help you concentrate, place it close to your desk, or wherever you need to concentrate. If you bought rose quartz to improve your self-esteem, keep it in your bathroom to learn to love your body, in the living room to spread gentleness around the room or in the bedroom to harmonise

your relationship with your significant other. For example, I placed an amethyst on my desk to help me concentrate when I wrote this book!

2. CAN I KEEP MY STONES WITH ME ALL THE TIME?

Yes, you can keep your stones on you all day and all night. This is even recommended with stones that act slowly, like agate. However, red stones should be avoided at night, as they are energising. But once again, the best thing to do is to try, and you'll see what works for you! From time to time, make an effort not to carry any stones with you in order to familiarise yourself with your body's own energy again, without any change being made by a crystal. This is absolutely necessary to redirect your practice as the weeks go by.

3. DO I HAVE TO CHANGE STONES EVERY DAY?

No. Working with your crystals will generally take several days. For slower stones, it may take a few weeks before you feel any real change. By reading these words, the most impatient among you may feel discouraged, but we are talking about energies here, about products offered by Nature, not the immediate gratification that defines our current society. Take some time off, slow down, connect with Nature. This spiritual journey often comes with environmental awareness and a desire to get back to Nature.

4. CAN I CHANGE STONES EVERY DAY?

If you don't feel like keeping the same stone on your person for several days in a row, then yes you absolutely can. Just make sure not to do this with stones that act slowly, or you may not draw any benefit from them.

5. I LISTEN TO MY INTUITION AND OBSERVE MYSELF

I recommend several times in this book that you keep a journal, a little notebook in which you write down your physical and non-physical sensations. Once you have spent a few hours and/or a few days wearing the same stone, take the time to ask yourself whether you feel something, anything at all. If you notice that the problem for which you chose your stone has improved, decide if you feel the desire to keep working with it. It's by listening to yourself attentively that you will be able to build your practice.

6. I TAKE TIME FOR MONTHLY INTROSPECTION

I recommend that at least once a month you make a little appointment with yourself. Write it down in your agenda: the first Wednesday of the month from 6pm to 7pm, for example, you will be there ONLY for yourself. Besides all the benefits provided by simply making yourself your number one priority, this monthly appointment will enable you to do some introspection, which is absolutely necessary for any

I trust myself

In modern spirituality, the plethora of advice we hear around us (in personal development books, in magazines, on the internet, on social media, etc.) is often contradictory and makes no sense. My advice: listen to your **intuition**. Keep a **critical mind** and trust what you feel. Don't hesitate to get information from different sources (see Digging Deeper on page 140).

My priority: me!

We ask stones to heal our energy, to realign us, to offer us a feeling of well-being, joy, or to absorb our stress, our pain, or sadness... They are saddled with a heavy responsibility, but be careful; as with any other therapy, this work has to be supported with mindfulness. If you are exhausted and you've been carrying stones to get your motivation back, but you're living in the fast lane without changing any of your habits, there's a strong chance that lithotherapy will not be enough. If you are tired, your body is asking you to slow down and rest, at least occasionally. The ideal stone will ultimately be the one that helps you make yourself the priority, and not the one that will temporarily mask the symptoms.

personal and spiritual change. This time is about listening to yourself (regardless of whether you choose to write during this time). Do you feel tired? Defeated? Demotivated? Joyful? Whatever the answer may be, ask yourself why. Based on this "why", you will be able to choose your stones and continue working with them.

7. I MIX INTUTION WITH EXPERIENCE

For stones to be able to continue offering you their supportive energy, you have to take care of them. Purifying, recharging and storing stones are little things that will become automatic in your practice. There are several methods, and I cover some of them in the following pages and invite you to try them to create your own experience. You will then be able to choose the one that speaks to you. In my opinion, there is no bad way to do this.

In this regard, you should beware of unscrupulous salespeople who swear to you that stones can only be purified using Himalayan pink salt, which they are happy to sell to you at a high price. Crystals, which were here long before us, don't need us as much as we would like to think. My clients often tell me that they feel lost in the wealth of information available on the internet about the purification of stones, so on the following pages you will find some straightforward advice.

Cleansing

Cleansing is an integral part of working with crystals. It will be a lot harder for them to help you benefit from their energy if they are "exhausted". When you cleanse them, you're giving them a new start, back to square one! There are many methods for this, which I will explain below.

1. SMOKE CLEANSING

I am starting with this method first because it's the one that I use. Smoke cleansing is a process in which a room or the surrounding of an object, in this case a stone, is filled with smoke. This can be done in various ways.

★ **Smudge sticks** The first way to cleanse a stone (and probably my favourite) is to light what is called a "smudge stick" (or cleansing stick), which is most often composed of branches of assembled and tied white sage (as in the photograph below). The Latin name for sage, which was used by Indigenous American populations, First Nations and the Celts, is *salvia*, which means "to heal" or "to save". When we burn sage, we also promote the healing of our own energy. In practice, you simply light the end of the stick, blow on the flame and let the smoke form. By moving your stones one by one through this smoke, you cleanse them of any

energy that they have accumulated from being near you – this does not necessarily mean negative energy. This can include vibrations or an emotional overload. Once you have cleansed the stones, you can take this stick through your home and wave it around yourself in order to

gain greater mental clarity and purify your energies and those of your house.

★ **How to make a smudge stick** You will find sage very easily in crystal shops. But if you have a garden or the space to have pots outside, plant some white sage, green sage, thyme, rosemary, lavender, etc. When your plants are fully grown, cut a few stems of each and let them dry upside down. Wrap the herbs together with some string and then tie a knot after pulling the string tight (really tight!). Let it dry for a few weeks. That's it! This form of cleansing, which is the most ethical of all, will enable you to get in closer touch with Nature: well-being and deep-rooting guaranteed!

★ **Incense** The process is exactly the same as for smudge sticks. However, the incense sticks that we generally use require

a great deal of transformation. The incense will have different properties depending on the one you choose. For example, some are made from lavender powder and have relaxing properties. Others are more dedicated to the elevation of the energies in the room, thanks to plants such as rhodiola rosea or palo santo. There are several forms of incense: sticks, cones, grains to be burned on hot coals, powders, etc. But they all have the same smoke cleansing potential, because they all emit a similar smoke. You will easily find incense in crystal shops.

2. SOUND

Another type of purification without any impact on the environment is sound therapy. The vibrations produced by sound can purify a room, object or person. If you ever have

Palo santo, the sacred tree

You may have heard of palo santo, a type of tree from Peru whose name means "sacred wood". When burned, this natural incense gives off a smoke with a bewitching smell. Unfortunately, this species has become a victim of overconsumption. For this reason, I do not recommend using palo santo for regular stone cleansing. If you are lucky enough to have some, use it sparingly, during your rituals or on an occasional basis. Honour and respect this tree.

the chance to participate in a Tibetan bowl guided meditation, I strongly recommend that you give it a try! It is a very special and amazing experience.

★ **Tibetan bowls** Fold a small piece of cloth, place it in the bottom of the Tibetan bowl, then add one or more stones and let them sing! This pure sound will cleanse your crystal. In some shops, the salespeople do this before they even give you your stone! You can find Tibetan bowls in most specialist shops or on the internet. However, I strongly recommend trying out a Tibetan bowl in person. A connection is created with this energy object, so it can be very useful to test it before buying it.

★ **Chimes** Chimes are another way to obtain a cleansing sound vibration. There are many different brands. You may even already have some at home. Don't hesitate to ring them mindfully right above your stones, and to state your intention of cleansing them. This works very well!

★ **Mantras** Perhaps you have already heard people chanting the mantra "OOOOMMM", a sound that is chanted or pronounced by making a particular vibration. The sound "OM", for example, connects us to the earthly vibration. It is considered to be the first syllable formed by a human being. While seated, try chanting this sound with the intention of cleansing the stone that you are holding in your hands. You can also chant "ganesha sharanam", a mantra that honours Ganesh, the god of wisdom and who removes obstacles, while holding a citrine in your hands, which promotes abundance in your life. This method, in addition to cleansing your crystals, will allow you to rebalance your chakras. There are many other mantras to chant in Sanskrit, but you can also invent your own and put your own intention into them.

3. MAGNETISM

We all have the power of magnetism. Now I'm not saying that it is possible for anyone to become a magnetiser and heal people with just a snap of the fingers, not by a long shot! On the other hand, we can all cleanse our stones thanks to *our* magnetism.

Have a try: Take a stone in your hands, take the time to focus on yourself and imagine a white light emanating from your hands. You may feel tingling, heat, or maybe nothing at all for the first few times, and that's not a problem! Once the light is present, visualise it cleansing your crystal, filling it completely. You will feel when this work is done.

Magnetism is a wonderful way to gain a deep connection with your stone. However, this method can be a little long if one wants to cleanse all of the crystals at the same time!

4. WATER

You can also cleanse your stones by running water over them or by leaving them for a few hours in a glass filled with water. Personally, I don't recommend this method, because I prefer smoke cleansing. Many stones do not tolerate water well (selenite, sulphur, pyrite, haematite, malachite, azurite, celestite and more!). Check before trying this method. However, if you are lucky enough to live near a source of fresh water (lake, river, etc.), don't hesitate to make a list of stones that have no trouble with this process and use it regularly. In addition to being purified, they will be filled with the earth's energy.

What happens if my stone is uncleansed?

Simply put, it will not give you its energy anymore. For example, I have a citrine ring on one of my fingers. It is magnificent, but I wear it more out of habit and pleasure than for the superb properties of the stone, which is so small that I would have to cleanse it every day! You can wear a stone that has not been regularly cleansed, but remember that it will be devoid of its energy.

Recharging

The recharging of crystals, which follows their cleansing, consists of filling the stone with energy again. All lithotherapists agree on this principle. As with cleansing, I invite you to choose the method that seems the most efficient to you.

1. IN THE SUN AND UNDER THE MOON

The first method consists of exposing the stones for a few hours to the light of the sun or the moon. Some people say that depending on the stone, the sun may be preferable to the moon, or vice versa. Regardless, make sure not to leave your crystals under strong sunlight, as some stones will have a tendency to lose their brightness in the sun – particularly quartz, but also amethyst and agate.

2. ON QUARTZ GEODES

This is my favourite recharging method. Simply place your stones, bracelets, pendants, etc. on a quartz geode (amethyst, rock crystal, etc.). Leaving them there for a few hours allows them to recharge.

3. IN THE EARTH

You can also dig a small hole in the ground and place your stones there for a few weeks before digging them up again. They will then be recharged thanks to the energy of the earth. This is the method that I recommend to people who

tell me that they don't feel anything from a crystal anymore, and when cleansing doesn't help. When a stone has been worn for several years, we can also consider that it has given us all the energy it could. If the last solution doesn't help, I recommend returning the stones back to Nature for good.

Make recharging a magical time

Personally, I make recharging a real ritual. I wait for summer, I go to a calm place (if you are lucky enough to have a garden, no need to go any further!), I thank my stone, I sing, I dance, I play music... whatever inspires me that day. I then place the stone in the earth and I go away with a smile on my face. You can also place it in a lake, on a beach or in a river – there are no rules for returning your stone back to Nature.

Storage

It is very likely that you will soon have (or already have) a nice collection of stones. Be careful not to overconsume. Remember that collecting crystals will not help you; working with them will! Here is some advice on keeping them in the best possible conditions.

1. SEPARATE YOUR STONES

Make sure to separate tumbled stones from raw stones. The raw stones could scratch the polished stones. Also remember to put very fragile stones, like selenite and raw malachite, in a cloth bag. Stones that can be scratched by your fingernails deserve very special attention.

2. AVOID STRONG, DIRECT LIGHT

Crystals don't like the sun very much; some of them will whiten if they are regularly exposed to it. So make sure to keep all your stones in a place where they are protected from strong direct light. I keep my tumbled stones in a transparent box because I like to look at them, but I put it far from the window in a place that is relatively dark in my apartment. As for my raw stones, they are stored in a lovely wooden box that I picked up at a flea market.

3. RECHARGE YOUR UNUSED CRYSTALS

According to some spiritual beliefs, certain shapes give off strong energy, capable of healing and connecting the person who takes interest in them to the Universe. The **flower of life** (shown in the photograph opposite), **Metatron's Cube** (above right) and **spirals** are just a few examples.

It might be interesting to print whatever symbol you choose on the medium of your choice – a sheet of paper, wood, cloth, etc. – to recharge your stones. Place them on it and state your intention of finding them recharged when you return.

You can also buy an **abalone shell** or a **scallop shell,** leave your crystals in it and state your intention of recharging them. Scallop shells are easy to find at any large supermarket. As for abalone shells, many specialist shops sell them.

SOS, my stone is gone!

When working with your stones, you will certainly break some and lose others. That's perfectly normal, no cause for panic! According to the beliefs of witches, there is a reason why this happens.

1. MY STONE IS BROKEN

Your stone "jumped" out of your pocket and broke in half? It slipped out of your hand and fell on the floor? You knocked it off the shelf? These different situations will definitely happen to you! To know what to do with the broken stone, start by looking at the break.

★ **If the stone is broken in half** (especially if it is a tumbled stone), this means that your stone probably has nothing left to offer. It has no more energy. It's time to give it back to Nature. If you don't have the heart to part with it, make sure to store it away from your other tumbled stones, as its broken edges could scratch stones that aren't as hard. Be careful, since a broken tumbled stone is almost always a sharp stone! Watch out for your fingers.

★ **If the stone is cracked**, and not completely broken, it can continue to work. It is a warning to let you know that it is almost at the end of its useful life. However, if you bought your stone already cracked, it may simply be a naturally-occurring ridge in the stone, in which case you can consider it as perfectly usable.

2. I LOST MY STONE

You've been looking everywhere, really everywhere, and you just can't find your stone... And you loved it so! I know the feeling, clients come in regularly and tell me the same thing, either in the shop or via social media.

In this case, it is said that you didn't really lose your stone, but rather your stone ran away from you. According to the beliefs of witches, we consider that if you can't find it, there's a reason! Maybe it doesn't have any more energy to give, maybe your work with it is over, maybe you don't need its properties anymore... The funny thing is that these stones sometimes reappear when we need them again!

Stones and washing machines...

Washing your stone in the washing machine... it's a problem that could happen to you if you forget to empty your pockets! Though some stones don't like water (see page 80), others will be just fine! We could even consider that they've been cleansed. But don't make it a habit in any case.

Black tourmaline

✦ **Chakra:** root
✦ **Colour:** black, sometimes with white inclusions
✦ **Keywords:** purification, anchoring, protection, action

Black tourmaline is an excellent stone for anchoring. It pushes our energy into the root chakra, offering its bearer a clearer and deeper connection with the earth. It allows us to connect to the earth and receive its teachings in a fluid manner. Its effect on energy enables it to absorb very negative surrounding energies. In my opinion, most of our bottlenecks or blockages come first and foremost from a Muladhara (root chakra) imbalance: it's the foundation of all the chakras, so if it isn't balanced, the others chakras can't be balanced either.

It is a powerful stone that, when well cleansed, purifies our energy, eliminates blockages and transforms very heavy energies into lighter, easier to handle energies. It reveals solutions to our problems and helps us have confidence in ourselves, while reducing the fear of taking action. It is excellent for anyone with passive tendencies.

How is it used?

Black tourmaline will be perfectly at home at the entrance to your house. A large block will offer protection and absorb negative energies that you have brought back with you from outside. You can also wear a bracelet or carry

a tumbled stone in your pocket to promote anchoring in the present moment. Tourmaline must be cleansed regularly, as it is a very absorbent stone.

Obsidian

✦ **Chakra:** root
✦ **Colours:** black, mahogany or snowflake, sometimes with golden streaks
✦ **Keywords:** purification, introspection, blockages

Obsidian is an extremely powerful stone that acts very quickly. It is said that you can't hide anything from it and that it inevitably reveals blockages or bottlenecks (even very old ones), defects, weaknesses and dark sides. It promotes introspection and enables realisations, the desire to seek out the truth and to feel better across the board. It forces us to grow up, to mature and to overcome self-destructive behaviours. No stone is bad, but obsidian has a tendency to bring out emotions that we have refused to experience. It is therefore an excellent stone if you are ready to do some work to understand the source of your stress or your lack of self-confidence.

Which obsidian should I start with? The black one is the strongest. To begin, I recommend mahogany obsidian or snowflake obsidian, which have a more gentle effect.

How is it used?

Due to its strength, I recommend that you begin by wearing it for one day, when you are at home, as obsidian can bring out strong emotions. Take time to listen to your sensations, to your feelings, and as soon as the effect seems too strong for you, put the stone aside. Start by

working with it for only a few hours. Little by little, you will be able to increase the time that you spend with its energy.

Carnelian

+ **Chakras:** sacral or root, depending on the colour
+ **Colours:** orange, red
+ **Keywords:** anchoring, vitality, motivation, creativity

Carnelian anchors our energies and enables your lower chakras (root, sacral) to be more balanced. It provides vitality and motivation, stimulates creativity and encourages you to launch into new projects with courage and desire. It invites you to have faith in yourself and dispels apathy and fear of failure. It also improves analytical ability and clarifies our perception of things.

It is a very positive stone that dispels superfluous, brooding thoughts and positively stimulates the mind if it is lethargic. It banishes negativity and anger. It makes it possible to feel more comfortable with the cycle of life and the acceptance of death. It supports the finding of joy again after depression. If we are affected by childhood experiences or were subject to mistreatment (regardless of the person or context), it helps us move on and turn the page, thus offering a new life. It is also reputed to improve fertility and promote fulfilling sexual relationships.

How is it used?

If you seek vitality or motivation on a daily basis, I suggest you try a bracelet, which you can put on as soon as you wake up and even keep on in the shower – you can also keep a small tumbled

stone in your pocket during the day. If you use carnelian for its properties at work, choose a large stone to place on your desk, just next to you. To promote fulfilling relationships, particularly with your significant other, it would fit perfectly at home in the bedroom (or the place where you spend the most time together).

97

Jasper

- ✦ Chakras: root, sacral, solar plexus, depending on the colour
- ✦ Varieties and colours: mookaite, red, dalmatian, leopard
- ✦ Keywords: protection, motivation, balance, anchoring, organisation

The property shared by all jaspers is protection. This stone anchors energies in the root chakra and in the earth, making us feel more confident in our physical body. It is a great help at times of intense stress and absorbs negative energy. It is very balanced, allowing us to be neither too emotional nor too action-oriented all the time: it provides harmony across the board. Jasper is perfect for anything work related, as it promotes organisation and bestows determination. It makes it easier to think and stimulates us to put our ideas into action. It is excellent for daring to take the first step and promotes altruism. When placed in the bedroom, it stimulates sexuality.

Which jasper should I choose? Red jasper offers motivation and momentum. It is ideal if you are tired and boosts health. It also helps us remember our dreams. Mookaite jasper is perfect for new experiences, because it pushes us to calmly leave our comfort zone. It encourages mental flexibility and when making decisions, it reveals all our options so that we can choose the right solution.

"Jasper" comes from the Greek iaspis and the Latin jaspidem, which mean "speckled stone".

How is it used?

Jasper is ideal to carry in your pocket, as close as possible to the root chakra, regardless of what you may be using it for. You can also choose a larger piece to place on your desk. In case of intense stress, keep a relatively large tumbled piece close at hand.

Tiger's eye

✦ **Chakras:** solar plexus and root
✦ **Colours:** brown and yellow
✦ **Keywords:** protection, anchoring, psychic gifts, self-confidence, balance

Tiger's eye allows us to anchor spiritual energy in its earthly reality. It is said to promote awareness and psychic gifts. It is reputed to be protective, particularly thanks to its anchoring capacity. It is very useful when working on projects, as this stone helps to clarify and reach objectives. It makes it possible to really commit oneself, helping desire and changes to take root, but also enables us to take into account and summarise all of the available information. It is perfect for people who are stubborn or too proud, as it helps us understand when we are a source of conflict, and to make the connection between our needs and those of others in order to tend towards balance. It also has the ability to promote self-confidence, consciousness of our own value, talents and abilities and unblocks creativity. Finally, it balances dualities, particularly the feminine and masculine.

How is it used?

If you are using it to anchor yourself in the present moment, try carrying some tiger's eye near your root chakra, in your pocket or on a bracelet. If your objective is commitment, organisation or the completion of projects, a tumbled stone

in your pocket or a pebble placed on your desk would be perfect!
For self-confidence, a pendent worn at the level of the solar
plexus chakra would be just the thing.

Natural citrine

♦ **Chakras:** solar plexus
♦ **Colour:** translucent yellow to dark honey
♦ **Keywords:** joy, optimism, luck, abundance, self-confidence, creativity

Natural citrine is an extremely warm stone that transforms negative energy (that comes from inside or from an outside source) into positive energy. It is very energising for the person carrying it! It is said that it has the ability to attract abundance, prosperity, riches and success, and that it also invites us to share. It pushes us to feel full of joy and to encourage joy around us. It is an excellent stone for dealing with melancholy, as it allows us to look to the future with optimism. It is very good for working with fears and phobias, as it calls us to inner peace. It offers deep-rooted self-confidence, keeps self-destructive tendencies at bay and makes it easier to express ourselves through creativity. It also reinforces concentration. Finally, it promotes intuition.

How is it used?

Citrine has many uses. A tumbled stone you can grab hold of in your pocket to make up for a lack of self-confidence when needed. When worn as a long necklace that ends at the level of the solar plexus, it's good for long-term work, in particular if you are trying to distance yourself from your self-destructive tendencies or your phobias. At home, a piece of raw citrine

Don't confuse natural citrine with heated citrine, which is actually amethyst that has been heated. It can be recognised because its colour is more orange and darker than natural citrine. It is also less expensive and has a much weaker effect.

(even heated) placed in the left corner farthest from your front door will enable you to attract abundance to your home.

Rose quartz

✦ **Chakra:** heart
✦ **Colour:** translucent pink
✦ **Keywords:** love, self-love, gentleness, goodwill, harmony, affection

Rose quartz is a must have; if I could only keep one stone, this would be it. It gives off an energy that is full of gentleness and peace. It's ideal for people who need to be reassured and is very comforting for children. As the stone of unconditional love, quartz affects the goodwill that we show ourselves and the compassion we offer to others. It is very useful for heartbreak; it helps us to let go of pain from the past and heals emotional deficiencies.

How is it used?

A large piece of raw rose quartz placed in a room helps with restorative sleep, even for children, as it is a gentle stone that gives off pleasant energy. In the living room, it helps people to get along. In the bathroom, it works on self-love, particularly if you have trouble loving your physical body. Rose quartz is also perfect for getting through existential crises, like that of adolescence. For this, the best thing is to wear it as a pendant near the heart, but a tumbled stone in your pocket works too.

To work more intensely, you can wear a bracelet. To heal the heart, wear a pendant for a long period of time directly over the heart chakra.

Green aventurine

Chakra: heart
✦ Colour: green
✦ Keywords: gentleness, comfort, couple, grieving, decisions

Green aventurine is perfect for promoting leadership qualities. It encourages perseverance, increases creativity and allows us to consider all the possibilities available to us, while paying special attention to proposals that come from others. It facilitates compassion, empathy and openness to other people. It helps us look back into the past to understand the source of negative feelings or self-destructive behaviour. It calms anger, irritation and helps us get past an injured ego and return to our heart, where we always find sincerity. It provides gentleness and comfort, and helps us heal the heart. It is said that it is useful for people with migraines and that it brings prosperity.

I've discussed green aventurine here, but this stone is available in other colours, which all act on a different chakra by offering additional properties (I warned you, lithotherapy is a broad field!).

How is it used?

Green aventurine is perfect when worn at the level of the heart chakra. You can also keep it in the form of a pebble or a tumbled stone in your pocket, where you can grab onto

it whenever you feel anger taking over. To work on prosperity, try wearing it as a bracelet on the left wrist. To work on the throat chakra or on an over-active mind, blue aventurine is preferable. If you lack confidence in your ability to make the right decisions, yellow aventurine is excellent!

Rhodonite

+ **Chakras:** heart and root
+ **Colours:** pink, streaked or speckled with black
+ **Keywords:** panic attack, anchoring, self-love, reconciliation, past injuries, mantras

Rhodonite is an emotionally balancing stone. Its pink colour speaks to the heart chakra, its black colour to the root chakra. It supports love and kinship, and enables us to care for emotional shocks. It reactivates the heart chakra and purifies it, helping us to realise that we are being emotionally self-destructive or in a co-dependent relationship. It eliminates past injuries and transforms the remaining emotions into something more positive. It facilitates reconciliation and helps us get over a betrayal or the pain of being abandoned. By promoting self-esteem and forgiveness, it is perfect for taking responsibility, particularly in our relationship with our significant other. It is a stone that balances yin and yang, revealing both sides of a problem. This stone is ideal for meditation, which it intensifies, and during rituals, especially if you like to chant mantras.

How is it used?

Rhodonite can be worn as a pendant to work on the purification of the heart chakra and forms of self-sabotage. It is also perfectly at home in your pocket, near your root chakra, to re-anchor in the present moment and to make it easier to let

The name "rhodonite" comes from the Greek rhodon, which means "rose". In ancient times, giving rhodonite was proof of friendship. It was popular with travellers, because it protected against attacks by highway robbers.

go. If you sometimes have panic attacks, having a small purified rhodonite stone in your bag is an excellent habit. Grab onto it whenever you feel your anxiety rising.

Aquamarine

✦ Chakras: heart and throat
✦ Colours: sky blue or green
✦ Keywords: communication, self-expression, courage, stress, intuition

Aquamarine is an excellent stone to fight stress – it acts like a real anxiety medication. It harmonises surrounding energies and gives courage. It gets rid of superfluous thoughts, clarifies perception and dispels confusion. It is also a stone that helps us take responsibility and encourages tolerance (towards ourselves and towards others). It offers considerable clairvoyance in terms of life and events, by pushing aside fears that obstruct our vision and increasing sensitivity. It helps us to connect with our intuition. It's perfect for meditation as it allow us to see beyond what we think, and to have faith in humanity. It is also excellent when we have a hard time communicating, talking about ourselves or our feelings. It enables us to start communicating with someone again when dialogue has been impossible.

How is it used?

Ideally you should wear it between the throat and the heart chakras, as a pendent or necklace of beads, to open your intuition and clairvoyance. Use a tumbled stone to keep in your hand to deepen meditation. An average-sized raw stone

Its name comes from the Latin *aqua marina*, *which means "seawater". In the middle ages, aquamarine was worn as a necklace to relieve toothache.*

(5cm/2in) would be perfect placed on a desk or table to promote friendly communication. Finally, in the event of stress, you should opt for a bracelet, possibly combined with a tumbled stone in your pocket, which is easy to grab.

Angelite

- ✦ **Chakra:** throat
- ✦ **Colour:** sky blue
- ✦ **Keywords:** peace, kinship, communication, perception

Angelite, as its name implies, offers its bearer a more intense connection with the world of angels, the invisible world, the Universe. It is very strongly related to subtle perceptions, encouraging us to feel them more strongly. It protects the body, living environment and physical reality of these worlds, enabling an exchange of healthy and positive energies.

This very gentle stone drives us to be more compassionate towards ourselves and others. It offers strong feelings of peace and security, enabling deep healing. It opens up the throat chakra, allowing us to dare to affirm our own truth, regardless of the consequences. It has a reputation for making it easier to understand maths and astrology.

How is it used?

Ideally, it should be worn as a pendant over the throat chakra, especially if you are using this stone for communication, and it will open you up to your own truth. A pebble to be carried in your pocket during longer periods of time will also work very well, particularly if you are trying to obtain deep healing.

"Angelite" comes from the Greek anhudros, which means "without water". It was chosen in 1804 by the mineralogist Abraham Gottlob Werner to highlight the absence of water in the composition of the stone.

Celestite (or celestine)

- Chakras: throat and third eye
- Colour: translucent sky blue
- Keywords: peace, kinship, communication, perception, harmonious relationships, spirituality, awakening

An excellent stone when you are at the beginning of your spiritual development, celestite drives us to connect with elevated vibrations and to make our practice meaningful. It promotes clairvoyance and helps us remember our dreams to extract messages from them. It is also known for healing the aura and establishing a connection with the Universe. This crystal attracts luck, brings balance and harmony and helps us maintain them in the long term. It is useful to cure periods of stress. It is also an excellent stone for breathing new life into contentious relationships or offering a neutral environment for negotiation and heated discussions. It enables us to trust the Universe and life and thus to experience a certain inner peace. It soothes the spirit and any worries we may have and promotes fluidity of thoughts and words. It is also perfect for meditation.

How is it used?

When used for clairvoyance, to elevate the energies of a place or to connect with the Universe, you should ideally use a raw stone. Place the stone in front of you or where you practice meditation, your rituals or your introspection. When used to seek out harmony or to avoid stress, a tumbled stone in your pocket would be perfectly fine.

"Celestite" comes from the *Latin* coelestis or caelestis, *which* means *"celestial"*. It is also called *"angel stone"*.

Lapis lazuli

✦ **Chakras:** throat and third eye
✦ **Colour:** navy blue with small golden inclusions
✦ **Keywords:** spirituality, truth, relationships, responsibilities, anger

This stone strongly stimulates the third eye chakra, so be careful to stay well anchored when you use it. It also impacts the throat chakra, teaching us that we can make it through many situations thanks to dialogue. It promotes active listening and goodwill towards the person speaking to us. It releases all bottlenecks of this chakra, particularly things left unsaid and past anger and resentment, helping us to express our opinions and resolve conflicts. It supports relationships and enables us to create a connection of trust, in love or in friendship, by making it easier to express our feelings. It is perfect for anyone who has a hard time saying "I love you"! It encourages us to take control of our life, to live according to our own truth, while being aware of our own abilities. It amplifies thoughts and provides objectivity and mental clarity. It increases creativity. Finally, it is a stone of spiritual protection, which puts us in contact with our guardian angels and keeps any sort of curse at bay.

How is it used?

To work on communication, try doing a little meditation, lying in the sun with a tumbled lapis lazuli stone placed on the third eye chakra. It will work powerfully and quickly.

Its name comes from the Latin lapis, which means "stone" and the Arabic azul, which means "blue". The first deposits were found more than 6,000 years ago in Afghanistan!

Then have a writing session to put down on paper whatever you need to get out. Ideally, you should wear it as a pendant near the throat. You can also work more passively, by simply carrying a stone in your pocket.

Sodalite

✦ **Chakras:** throat and third eye
✦ **Colour:** primarily navy blue, sometime with white, red or black inclusions
✦ **Keywords:** spirituality, meditation, truth, fresh start

This very spiritual stone, particularly when used in meditation, allows us to understand the messages of the Universe and to bring them down to the physical realm. It encourages us to seek the truth, while remaining faithful to our convictions and our values. It promotes a healthy mind, easier comprehension in group settings as well as rational, objective and creative thought.

It calms panic attacks, instils true emotional balance and helps us talk about our feelings. It increases our self-respect and self-confidence and enables us to ignore the judgements of others. It invites us to look at the darker aspects of our personality with honesty and to accept them. Very useful for new beginnings, sodalite allow us to abandon obsolete thought patterns, upbringings or values that no longer work for us. It conveys flexibility of the mind and is perfect for those who need to control everything.

How is it used?

The best way to use it is to wear it as a pendant as close as possible to the throat chakra to express your truth, to make it easier to express your feelings and for anything

related to communication. If you sometimes have panic attacks, having a small purified stone in your bag is a good habit: grab onto it whenever you feel your anxiety rising. You can also carry a tumbled stone or wear a bracelet for longer work or to help make a fresh start!

Labradorite

◆ **Chakras:** throat and third eye
◆ **Colours:** grey to black, most often with green or blue streaks, sometimes orange, yellow or purple
◆ **Keywords:** spiritual protection, introspection, intuition, wisdom

Labradorite acts as a true energy shield all around the aura to block negative energy coming from other people. It also allows us to detach ourselves from what others think and to live our life fully, solely for ourselves.

This very spiritual stone encourages us to elevate our consciousness and to use our intuition. It highlights psychic gifts and simulates the art of being "at the right place at the right time". It helps us decode messages from our subconscious, making it easier to understand them. It is the perfect stone for working on our spiritual development, because it prepares the body and mind for change. It reinforces trust in ourselves and in the Universe and banishes insecurities and fears as well as past disappointments. It allows us to have new ideas and imagination. It is very useful for introspection sessions and invites us to forge a kind of intuitive wisdom.

How is it used?

If you work in a place where people confide in you a lot, or where you absorb the emotions of others, a relatively large labradorite placed in this area would be very useful. You can also carry a tumbled stone on your body. If you are very sensitive to energies, places with a lot of people can be exhausting; personally, I always wear a labradorite bracelet in this kind of situation. To promote work where intuition is important, wear a tumbled stone for a longer period of time.

Fluorite (or Fluorine)

✦ **Chakras:** heart, third eye and crown, depending on the colour
✦ **Colours:** translucent green, yellow, purple or blue
✦ **Keywords:** spirituality, protection, stress, intuition, organisation, concentration

Fluorite is a very spiritual stone that protects against outside influences. It helps us become aware of whatever has an oppressing hold on its wearer and to get rid of it! It purifies the aura and absorbs the body's negative energy and stress. It intensifies work with intuition and makes us more conscious of and open to the invisible world. It accelerates spiritual development and allows the mind to connect to the Universe. It organises learning and increases concentration; it is therefore suitable for anyone who is studying.

Fluorite structures daily life, emotions, plans, etc. It chases away small-mindedness and prejudice, leading to more interesting reflections. It is the stone of disillusion, it shines light on the truth.

Which colour should I choose? Green fluorite is perfect for facing emotional trauma; it cleanses the aura and sharpens our intuition so that the heart can make use of it. Yellow fluorite increases creativity and makes intellectual activities easier, especially in groups. Purple fluorite opens the intuition and makes it possible to enter into contact with the subconscious more easily. It is ideal when we are seeking spiritual progress.

How is it used?

To work on intuition, choose raw fluorite and place it in front
of you during your rituals and meditations. To work on stress
and purification on a daily basis, a tumbled stone in the colour
of your choice placed in your pocket is perfect! If you are
a student, choose a pebble placed right in front of you.
Cleanse the stone regularly.

Amethyst

- ✦ **Chakras:** third eye and crown
- ✦ **Colour:** purple of various shades, sometimes with white-coloured chevrons
- ✦ **Keywords:** intuition, aura, decisions, grief, anxiety

Amethyst is a very spiritual stone, that promotes the use of intuition and contact with our inner witch. It offers a feeling of serenity, gentleness and confidence. It promotes spiritual awareness and opens the door to another reality. It boosts altruism because it encourages us to be interested in others and to consider that we are all connected. Amethyst is excellent for meditation and activates and strengthens psychic gifts. It purifies the aura.

Amethyst allows us to manage an over-active or under-active mind, by soothing it or helping us to think constructively. It helps us feel less scatterbrained, more concentrated and in control of our abilities. It also invites us to make decisions using common sense and logic and by integrating new ideas more easily. It improves motivation and helps us set realistic objectives.

If we are going through a lot of ups and downs, it is our best ally. It helps us release anger, fear and sadness. It is very useful when learning to accept death and to grieve. It is a great help if you have insomnia caused by a hyperactive mind and keeps recurring nightmares at bay.

How is it used?

The best thing to soothe the mind is to lay down on the ground and place an amethyst directly on your third eye chakra. For everyday use, a bracelet is great, possibly combined with a tumbled stone to hold when you need motivation. For mediation and psychic gifts and to use amethyst in rituals, try a small raw stone, also called a druse, which you can place on the ground in front of you. Finally, to take advantage of its energy in an entire room, you can use a large geode.

Howlite

✦ **Chakra:** crown
✦ **Colour:** white with black stripes
✦ **Keywords:** soothing, stress, intuition, projection, patience, anger

Howlite is an extremely gentle and calming stone that immediately offers a soothing feeling. It helps us to fall asleep, particularly if one has insomnia related to mental hyperactivity. It is very spiritual and helps us connect with our inner wisdom and prepare to receive messages from the Universe and/or from our intuition. It makes it easier to access our past lives, particularly through working with dreams. With its gentleness, howlite teaches us patience, to control our anger and to take responsibility for our own emotions. It encourages us to be more tolerant, less critical and reinforces our positive personality traits. It helps us speak simply and calmly and encourages us to see things through to the end. It also helps us to organise our ideas and projects, to clearly state our ambitions and to trace a path to get there.

How is it used?

Wear a bracelet if your objective is to soothe. For sleep, you might try a tumbled stone placed under your pillow. For anything related to organisation or the planning of your dreams and objectives, opt for a stone that you can keep near you during your introspective sessions.

Its name was given as a tribute to the geologist Henry How, who did research on this stone. Indigenous Americans also called it "white bison stone", because it was as rare as white bison in South America.

Rock crystal
(or clear quartz)

✦ Chakras: all
✦ Colour: transparent
✦ Keywords: spirituality, psychic gifts, clarity, purity, great healer

This quartz, which is well known for its amplifying properties, is perfect in combination with other stones. It supports and amplifies their energies. Used alone, it makes the energy as pure as possible. It keeps away superfluous thoughts, offers very deep concentration and unblocks memories. Rock crystal, called "the great healer", is absolutely necessary for harmonising all your chakras.

It also brings you into contact with your psychic gifts and your soul, so that you can be in deeper harmony with your life's path and your spiritual goal. It is therefore a stone that upends the ego, allowing us to let go of what we think we know and what we think "we" are, to connect to something much greater.

How is it used?

To cleanse your various crystals, use rock crystal in the form of an open geode and place them inside. To amplify energies, there are several options. If you are wearing stones as bracelets, add a rock crystal bracelet. If you are keeping tumbled stones in your pocket, then adding a small tumbled

rock crystal to your synergy would be a perfect fit. I recommend placing a point of rock crystal turned towards Nature or set upright towards the Universe where you have your rituals or your meditation.

129

Moonstone

- ✦ Chakras: root, sacral, third eye, depending on the colour
- ✦ Colours: orange, grey or white
- ✦ Keywords: cycles, new start, stress, intuition, subconscious, empathy, emotions

Moonstone is particularly connected to the various cycles: the cycle of life and rebirth and death, for example, which makes it perfect for new beginnings. It helps us let go of the past. It has the power to connect us to the cycle of the seasons, the cycle of the Moon and to the menstrual cycle, which it strongly influences. In men, it promotes the awakening of feminine energy (creativity, sensitivity, gentleness, intuition). It is a stone that soothes strong emotions but increases sensitivity and empathy.

Very spiritual, it enables us to connect with our intuition and our subconscious to decode its messages. When worn during a full moon, it sends many messages in the form of dreams. It can also be used to develop your psychic gifts and promote clairvoyance. It makes it possible to reduce stress and to allow obsolete practices or habits to die out. It brings deep emotional healing. It calms hyperactive children.

How is it used?

To work with your feminine energy, a very interesting ritual is to lay down and place a moonstone on your sacral chakra (about two fingers below the navel). This is also a good practice to ease menstrual pain. You can wear it as a pendent or carry it as a tumbled stone, but keeping it directly near your sacral chakra is key!

Agate

- ✦ **Chakras:** all, depending on the colour
- ✦ **Colours:** exists in every colour
- ✦ **Keywords:** balance, inner peace, motivation, stress, abundance

Agate is a very balancing stone across the board. It encourages tact and emotional, physical and intellectual balance. It promotes anchoring and focusing on ourselves. This slow-acting stone should be carried with you for long periods of time. It enables us to find practical solutions, by promoting a critical spirit, love of truth and analytical capacities. All varieties of agate invite us to accept starting again, to start new adventures and to learn the lessons of the past.

Which colour should I choose? Blue agate is the stone of inner peace; it calms and soothes. It elevates our consciousness to higher planes and connects us to the collective consciousness, to the unity that surrounds us all. Red agate encourages us to act, it offers motivation and stability over the long term to reach our objectives. Botswana agate is very beneficial in helping smokers to quit. It encourages us to find solutions and not to play the victim. It helps us explore our own creativity. Moss agate allows us to feel connected to Nature; it also attracts abundance and riches. It helps us build self-confidence and reduces stress.

How is it used?

Agate is a stone that acts gently, so it should be worn for long periods of time. Don't hesitate to keep it with you for several weeks; it would certainly be easiest to have it in bracelet form so that you can keep it on at night and in the shower. But be careful: if your bracelet is made of red agate, sleeping with it may be difficult, as it pushes the body to be active. Try it and adjust your practice.

Malachite

✦ **Chakras:** heart, third eye
✦ **Colours:** dark and light green
✦ **Keywords:** transformation, harmony, intuition

Malachite is a stone that amplifies energies, both positive and negative. That's why it is considered to be a powerful stone to be used with a few precautions. It is also a stone of transformation: it encourages us to take risks and to change whatever is blocking us in our progress (spiritual, physical, emotional, etc.). If we have undesirable connections or toxic relationships, it will bring them to the forefront so that we can get rid of them.

It is excellent for helping our heart align with what is around us, allowing us to open ourselves to unconditional and universal love. It develops empathy and promotes friendship. It also helps its bearer put into words his or her emotions and to let them out. Finally, malachite amplifies intuition and helps us enter into contact with the invisible realms.

How is it used?

Given the strength of malachite, you may want to start with a small tumbled stone and very conscious work. In meditation, connect with its energy and see what it brings out in you. This in itself can be an experience rich in emotions and feelings! You can then wear it, especially by your heart, to promote love and to help with the rebirth process.

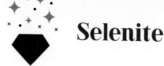

Selenite

+ **Chakras: crown and root**
+ **Colour: white**
+ **Keywords: light, peace**

Selenite is a very luminous stone. During energy work, it brings light while helping us stay fully anchored to the earth. It is also perfect for meditation, as it enables us to understand the messages that our subconscious is trying to share with us. It encourages deep inner peace, dispels mental confusion and allows us to understand things that are implicit and not clearly stated. It stabilises our emotions and calms people who are agitated.

How is it used?

To fill your home with gentleness and serenity, don't hesitate to invest in a selenite lamp or in a large block to be placed in the middle of a room. It is also said that to protect the home, you can place selenite stones in the four corners of a room. For its calming and soothing properties, I recommend a large pebble that you can hold in your hands during meditation (even for a short time!). It's life changing. It is also possible to work with selenite as a bracelet around your wrist or a tumbled stone in your pocket.

"Selenite" comes from the Latin *selenitis*, which means "moon". It is said that this stone comes from Selene, the Greek goddess of the Moon, of bounty and of goodwill.

In conclusion

I think it is important enough to say it again one last time: trust yourself. Learn from yourself, from your choices, from your intuition, from your feelings. You can be certain that each of your experiences with energy and stones will be constructive for what's to come. Don't hesitate to write down what you experience during this work in a journal; you will notice changes as the weeks go by.

I am thrilled to have been able to support you in your discovery of lithotherapy, which is now my daily life. If you want to continue reading or ask me any questions, feel free to contact me via my online shop or my Instagram account. I write short posts (in French) on a daily basis about crystals, spirituality, my spiritual life and many other things! I would be very happy to chat with you! You can also visit my shop in Loire-Atlantique, Western France. Here is all the useful information:

Mysticbox, 48, rue Georges Clemenceau
F-44150 Ancenis-Saint-Géréon

https://mysticbox.fr/ • @Mysticboxfr

I hope that you are motivated to add more mindfulness and attention into your energy well-being. I wish you an amazing walk along your spiritual path. Wherever it takes you, you can be sure that it will feel right!

Digging deeper

- *Crystal Power, Crystal Healing: The Complete Handbook*, Michael Gienger, Cassell, 2020

- *The Encyclopedia of Crystals*, Judy Hall, Fair Winds Press, 2013

- *The Chakra Project*, Georgia Coleridge, Aster, 2018

- *The Green Witch*, Arin Murphy-Hiscock, Adams Media, 2017

- *The Witch's Book of Self-Care*, Arin Murphy-Hiscock, Adams Media, 2018

- *Witch*, Lisa Lister, Hay House, 2017

Acknowledgements

With the heart chakra full of gratitude, I would like to thank Gregory, my spouse and co-worker in the company, who took care of the shop alone while I concentrated on writing this book, and who supported me from start to finish.

A big thank you to my family as well, for the unconditional and precious love that they have for me and the encouragements that they offer me daily, even when their beliefs and mine are different.

I would also like to thank Romane, Louise, Julie, Coralie, "Gergoire", Vanina, all these friends who supported and assisted me, each in their own way. Thank you for adding goodwill, humour, craziness, listening and wisdom to my life.

A very special thank you to the online and real-life community that follows Mysticbox; THANK YOU for giving me all these incredible experiences, you are what inspires me every day.

Finally, to Editions Larousse and Maud in particular: thank you for giving me this opportunity. What an incredible experience!

Claire Taupin runs her own crystal store and online store, Mysticbox. Having been on the spiritual path for several years, she is proud to call herself a witch. In *Crystals and Energies*, she is delighted to offer her advice on how to start or develop your practice with crystals.

Cristaux et Énergies first published in 2021 by Larousse
This English hardback edition published in 2022 by Quadrille

First published in 2022 by Quadrille, an imprint of Hardie Grant Publishing
52–54 Southwark Street
London SE1 1UN
quadrille.com

TEXT Claire Taupin
ART DIRECTION Géraldine Lamy
DESIGN Valentine Antenni

Images © Claire Taupin: p. 21, 23, 31, 32, 35, 37, 39, 40, 43, 45, 47, 49, 53, 55, 61, 63, 64, 67, 68, 74, 75, 76, 77, 79, 81, 83, 88, 93-137, 141, 142.
All other images are from © Shutterstock.

For the English language hardback edition:
MANAGING DIRECTOR Sarah Lavelle
COMMISSIONING EDITOR Sarah Thickett
DESIGNER Alicia House
HEAD OF PRODUCTION Stephen Lang
PRODUCTION CONTROLLER Lisa Fiske

The content of this book is the opinion of the author. No medical claims are made for the stones in this book and the information given is not intended to act as a substitute for medical treatment. The healing properties are given for guidance only and are, for the most part, based on anecdotal evidence and/or traditional therapeutic use. The advice in this book is intended solely for informational and educational purposes and not as medical advice. If in any doubt, a medical professional should be consulted.

Cataloguing in Publication Data: a catalogue record for this book is available from the British Library.

Text © Larousse 2021
Layout © Quadrille 2022

ISBN 978 1 78713 929 9
Printed in China

MIX
Paper from responsible sources
FSC
www.fsc.org   FSC™ C020056